A HORNET'S NEST OF BEES

Front cover photo:
This is composed of relatives on my father's side; the Hauser family
originated in the Berner Oberland region of Switzerland, with
descendants settling primarily in northern Wisconsin,
where this photo was taken.

BY THE SAME AUTHOR

Two Sisters (poetry)
The Message (poetry, with Jay Ramsay)
A Women's Guide To Saving The World
(collection of 'comments')

anthologies:
Cartwheels On The Faultline
Salt Water/Sweet Water
Sonoma Mandala
Tears in the Fence
Moor Poets II
Acumen

A HORNET'S NEST OF BEES

Karen Eberhardt Shelton

Earthkin Books

Published by EARTHKIN BOOKS, 2009

Typesetting: cover in Requiem
subsequent text in Baskerville
Cover layout designed by Steve Wall
Technical assistance from David Wheeler and John Elford
Funding assisted by Elizabeth Finn Trust

Printed and bound in Exeter, Devon, UK
by ImprintDigital on recycled paper

A catalogue record for this book
is available from The British Library

ISBN 978-0-9562874-0-3

Born in California, Karen Eberhardt Shelton first moved to England as a teenager, eventually married there and became a British subject. In 1999 she relocated permanently to the West Country where she works as a freelance journalist and author. She has written two books of poetry, been published in newspapers ranging from *The New York Times* to *The Guardian*, with an ongoing variety of freelance work appearing globally in magazines, newspapers and poetry publications. Her photography has been featured in two exhibitions and she was won several photography awards. A committed environmental activist, her goal is to set up an Eco-Trust for wildlife protection and the promotion of sustainable living, and do everything possible to encourage humans to nurture their interdependent relationship with the earth.

DEDICATION

To those I have been part of and they a part of me; to their lives
and spirits, their eyes and hearts and fleece, their legs and tongues
and tears, their growls and bleats and song . . to the still living ones,
our journey continues, and for those who are gone, the connections
and memories endure. (My father Del, mother Betsy, siblings Rosemary
and Jerome, daughter Asia, son Michael, my unforgettable dog, Camelot,
and a long line of greatly loved pets)

CONTENTS

CONTENTS (continued)

CONTENTS (continued)

REMEMBERING DAVID (1970)
(an artist who was the love of my life – the fabric of my days changed radically from this point onward)

A freedom, lightness, pollen in the veins
outstaring the sun
making silent hieroglyphics on the moon
sieving the wind with fingers
hair scented with frangipani and coppertone oil
your full-pooled brush-stroked eyes
calling with a compelling nod
calling without need of voice
summoning me to fling my body after yours
into the sea unclothed
unfettered by social blight or rules of form

You led me along grassways to rivers
through mud unafraid and willing
with never a can't do or won't or we shouldn't

This being free is a once-lived dream, a choice
of soul over mind and balanced breath
like the mist of waterfall
strong beneath the delicate imagery
saying no where flesh is unwilling
like the foetus I emptied out
because there was no plan

No to overly-sugared sentiments
yes to wings free-falling my poetry, your art
tears of parting tenderness
our hems not ready to be stitched as one
our shores separating
never to be walked by old shoes or joined hands

PRELUDE TO UNKNOTTING (1977)

How did he get to be this way?
Silly old warrior – maybe he rode
with Genghis Khan or Alexander –
superior, superlative and right.
Strange might of such men, ancestors,
genes, motives rising from complaints

Something comes between us
when I talk about where I am, a woman,
and he could help me, but then he'd be on the team
of savages ravaging me and the village –
innocent, he would insist, because he was one
of the men following orders – he is like that.
But the way of it goes far back
brick-on-brick and then the wall,
walls in every epoch, with some
called by other names

He was damaged too by an unnatural childhood
and his teacher's ticklish hand –
so many things to excuse him, and yes,
they're real, same as the things I claim,
we women and our abuse.
They are abused too.
So why the gap between us?

Meanwhile, it is now, this age.
I do my best to understand his sullen stance
beside the door when I ask for help
around the yard, if he could buy
our daughter shoes. He doesn't know;
I'll think about it. What's to think about?
Have we no hold on you,
separate as you are from life?

A MAN'S WRECKAGE (1978)

He is the Bedford-Stuyvesant of my mind.
Oh Nemesis! You five cobs-of-corn eater!
Single child of the smoking mother
child raised in criminal New York
where winter wasn't taught to nurture souls. . .
You lonely old wart
turned in like a sour toenail
a man who goes home to brood in the study
and pinch his psyche into silence
and leave me with mine

Old football game watcher!
stalwart with a mean streak who never
asks why are you crying? Will you be ok?

Took his father home drunk on the subway
and learned not to shed tears
walks off with a stiff jaw
fastidious keeper of the self-righteous moment
no pity in that granite face

Now I have to crawl back and be sorry
and worry and gnaw out my forgiving
Oh half-listener
drawing on the weapon of silence
rather than transmit a care

You stiff-spined, half-baked spirit
letting out rainbows only in rare patches
afraid to whisper your bruises
not showing, not wanting to know
stubborn as an old serpent who coldly
invents excuses for ignoring
his wife who, for now, lives in a shared space

OUR FLAPPING WALLS (1982)

This fabric house – to observers an awesome tent,
 this swooping white temple, this Bedouin refuge
thumping and cracking in the wind, cats piled round my feet
canopy poles creaking, front door a flapping sail.
I burn onions cooking on the tiny stove.
A small spider crawls across the base of an oil lamp
Molly Baa Baa, quiet dog, rests like slippers on my feet.
I live in this space where the language of California wind
lays its palms on walls no thicker than paper
and my ears are brushed by the taffeta-rustle of leaves
as though I am the tree they belong to;
this paper lantern protecting me from frost and rain
a thin uterine wall holding back the absolutes.
Even thunder and fog and August heat
respect this soft eggshell; as though the Tower of London
and Berlin Wall and ramparts on the Khyber Pass
were fatuous examples of trust in thick barriers.
All we need here in Sonoma county, me and these pets,
the man I married, a child soon to arrive from India,
are the basic pearls of who we are,
a solid care to breathe in only essentials.
This warm stomach of a feather-clad bird
will do the rest.

A NIGHT ON MY OWN (1983)

Water is back in the well
chickens are sleeping
the wind packs its little suitcase and leaves
new grape stalks are freed from the threat of nettles
dear Sand the dog farts

Water runs in the pipes again
I am alone on the hill
but still in the company of owls
and mites in the cat's ears
and Neruda, Rilke and Bly
good lamps and heaters.

Adrenalin throbs out of sight below
minds different from mine breaking glass
cutting fence, dumping bags beside the road
like dead skins and hatred

Cats of all ages surround me
and while the dishes sit drying
my eyelids draw to a close

HOW YOU SPEND A LIFE (1984)

Time melts like slabs of butter that drip
hours down passages of no return,
devouring weeks and months and years.
I hold soft baby hands
that grow before I've released them.
There are new robins, new holly, new winds and rain,
a nest of seventeen grey hairs beside the sink
plucked from my head like stalks of fading wheat.
I slowly float beneath my flannel sheet
and dreams gush faster than I can reach.
I twirl in the wake of rising sun
and find it wearing noon.
Then take the dog to run,
slipping in and out of shadows
and past hills that will soon be clothed in moonlight.
Next morning a regal stag glides through the dew
and nods to the fawns and new lambs,
then salutes the ancient ring of redwoods above his crown.
The earth cools like a lush fruitcake
whose raisins must eventually grow hard.
Star twitches of lustre flood prairies and Yosemite
when their infinite filaments penetrate the air.
I sit by a lamp thinking
through the Milky Way of space,
hearing wind rush all the way to Chicago and beyond.
A flicker of the clock presses my eyelids
as I resist the closure of the night.
I feel the old slowing that binds the world
into seeds of solemn new beginnings.
Before sleep holds me, I pray that I too will be included.

A FAMILY IN WINTER (1985)

Cold is coming from everywhere
streaming through outer space and the valleys
the bay leaves are drying
the desperate buy dyed flowers
my child wheezes in the night
like an accordion with a broken throat
Monday night football divides families
who separately devour chocolate and beer
frost lies so whitely dim in the morning
we wince to see it and clutch at our flannel sheets

Creeping down the drive in low gear
we pause for deer jolting on stiff knees
the cats press toward the glass
and pray with their cat paws
for doors to open

There is soup and smoke
rug tufts between our toes
you break ice in the water so sheep can drink
I watch for Halley's comet

We bargain with the wood to last
oh, never so cold a California!
Is this my childhood repeating
the same candles trembling
touch withheld in our home's draughts?

CAT BITE (1985)

Dark red stone bandage
contains my fingers.
I am stale bread on a white shelf.
If God in his gowns would pause,
I'd know my fate.
Beyond this room there is wind and radiance,
the seduction I crave
beyond IVs and heparin, tight sheets,
needles, swabs, nurse faces
changing like tides.
Lambs wait in the sun
where the peacock strolls,
bleating the old sound centuries removed
from this sterile ward of lame bodies.
Now, after the cat bite
I mark time, swelling and unswelling
with finger pain, soul pain
winging out of a green source
that glows where the window ends
and tries to bring new blood to my veins

DOG I

TRAVELLING SAND (1985)

Blond puppy from a London pet shop
straddles my lap as I sit overlooking the green
of Clapham Common. He turned out to be very small
but didn't bat a paw over riding in an airborne box
to New York where he learned to bark like a yankee

All those unflawed years – the coming and going
of catamarans and planes and cats and even a car-borne transition
across the whole of America to a pillow on the floor
of a fabric house. Oh, he gently barked, you should hear the story
in that. Until his kidneys failed and on September 6, 1985
he glided on deaf paws into the sleep that can't be stopped.

Then our lives together faded into history
as though he was a rich kind sultan and I part of his harem
except we were really just a woman and her sweet dog

DOG II

MOLLY BAA BAA AND THE 40 FLEAS (1990)

Woolly-black and soft and kind. Not a conqueror.
Not blind or thick; she simply loved her home
in every way and taste of it and me there for her when the sky
flicked with stars and the pair of us running together over and over
past the fragrant geography of our special spot
wrapped though with coyote brush, eucalyptus and oak
and faint scent of distant sea as flicks of salt in Baa Baa's coat.
No dog could complain or fret less. Modest lass and mother

happy to oblige in all weathers; a universal mop (even in appearance)
soaking up our flaws and love and negligence.
Even when I vanished into Sussex for a year
and came back to carers who said to no sign of her,
as though we had disappeared together into the hearts
of separate lives, except I fear Stuart the farmer shot her
and hid my love from me, and her fictitious fleas.

A HINT OF GRACE BEYOND THE AVERAGE DAY (1986)

Peacocks stand
like blue shadows on the roof
and she frets, watching
through a dawn bubble
drenched in acacia and dreams.

Her child will burst rumpled
through the door.
The house will straighten
its bones.
Should there be anything more
after tea and news and a folded smile?

Oh, after awhile the furrows
are smoothed;
the peacock's rainbow
goes pecking with the hens.
Thunder stomps far off
and the fault line in her heart
is temporarily repaired
with bagels and cream cheese.

A BREATH TO REMEMBER (1986)

This song holds a child and a lawnmower
and a swing dangling from the rafters
that bumps plants and a kitten
leaping at the child's feet.
A song is sung to praise this hour
of purple and green, layers of gold
long soft shadows and fading heat.
Now the child rests on my bare thighs
while I lie dreaming and absorbing
the sweet dizziness of this languid spell
before it seeps away into night's mouth.
Someone has control of the lawnmower
as it showers grass into the air
until the oxygen falls like confetti
and we all smell the green in our hair.
Goat bells tinkle like stars
wandering through the field
and their hymn gently tickles our ears.
This is a song that ends
only when the sun raises an arm
to its face and waves and drifts
silently to its own room to sleep.

PHOTOGRAPH OF MY EARLY SELF (1986)

Steps lead to a door, the grass
her years that went before, the mother's laugh
She has placed her feet in shoes, a father's shoes
appearing whitely big and new
Her arms are baby arms, muscles still asleep
The dark brown curly head is bent; it looks
for coordination in the toes. She chews her lip
the ruffles on her dress are soft and blue
The eyes of Mother watch – she's there
outside the frame, alert and full of care
The camera clicks, the air is frozen
for the child to see when grown;
a dozen seconds picked from summer's yield
the sundress sheathing innocence and dormant wit
each step travelled one by one within these shoes
from door to grass, to fit at last
in mother's lap, to sleep and own
her babyhood and what's to come

ADOPTION SEARCH (1986)

Today I may begin to find him
my one potato in a million rows.
He is darker, more like a beet
all these years growing in distant soil
in a life shielded from his roots.

I am his basic stalk, yet he hasn't found me,
hasn't look, hasn't seen, hasn't felt
me calling, hasn't ploughed
through these furrows of time
back to being my shoot
in the greenness of my freshly sown youth.
Son. First seed and only seed
out of season and transplanted
and somewhere still maturing
amongst the hills of string beans and oats.

ON THE NIGHT BEFORE MY SON COMES TO MEET ME
FOR THE FIRST TIME (1987)

What do I look for
beyond straining to see myself
more reverberating than a mirror
to feel the breath of an image
I could never imagine or show others

My body carried him kicking the first mile
away from my heart lest I disobey
my leaning for space and a foreign view of time
A village spangling strange words in the light
A red bus at Trafalgar Square
Chapattis and mangoes in the sooty dusk
A blue mosque, pure Swiss alps. . .
I expected such offerings
as my life's share
but was given only one cutting from the cloth

And I await this now, electrified
drumming my fingers on the tabletop
anxious, awed at the prospect
and nearly flawed into disbelieving and flight

My wet eyes will greet him
my mouth working
twenty five years later joy a tight coil
smarting like any poverty or denial
My heart inventing dialogue
that may dissolve into banality or jest. . .
Clothes meld with my body's damp chaos
as I cling to a mossy limb
straining to see him before he sees me

For it is this recognition
acknowledgment like a swan gazing for the first time
at its mature self
That makes the leaves tremble with me
whether from fear or fulfilment
only the wind knows

HAROLD DYING UNDER THE KITCHEN TABLE (1987)

Harold the peacock is under the big table in the kitchen
taking his leave of me and his wife Maude,
round-eyed in the faltering slide downward,
loitering like a plumed ghost on a mission
to some dark spot in the peacock world

He becomes light in his own heaviness
scalds the floor with his blue breast
like a dropped gem lying in dust

I work through the day picturing his ghost,
love flayed by the sight of his face
tears I can't contain curse the dying of birds
who still carry rainbows in their clothes

Does he feel death bending close in this busy room?
I act the mother of a pharaoh or priest
wearing iridescent long-tailed robes –
this most gentle mover of air and wings
touching the leaves of willow or northern lights
dancing beside his spectral throne –
not meaning to mock our busy pace
during the final hours he waits to disappear

I'm helpless about what to do besides stroke
his feathered patterns and watch submission
to his long passage dribble slowly from his beak

If there is truth in him, he will go tonight
and in the morning he'll be still, cold neck bent
in a final question mark. Then I will grieve most
and sing farewell to his soulful closing flight.

TALL BLOND SPARK (1988)

Rosemary is 44 all of a sudden
on July 1st when she opens her eyes
to look down at her body adding a year.
She ponders this while going
from room to room talking
to her bicycle and the cat
which never show signs of age
until shortly before death.
The universe notices these events.
Whoever increases or decreases
their sum total, and represents all life,
should know a reverberation echoes
in the forests and oceans, a cymbal
crashes on the doorstep of eternity
to remind God we are still
in the process of inventing our roles.

THIS SPECIAL ONE (1988)

He's a dog with mettle, even a nose for nettles.
He barks inside the house but never
raises his voice unnecessarily;
a series of wrummps to call for his pillow bed.
I sniff his cheek while he cradles his head
in my armpit, so calm and gentle a black saint,
an exemplary water lily on the vast pond of life.
But give him a rawhide chew for something to do
and relieve boredom, he'll sit up and vote,
as though this small thing was about managing a kingdom.

We have intimate discussions about unpaved roads
and pig's ears, leg lifts, walking in rain,
people's treatment of their unloved dogs (he doesn't want
to hear that); when I mentioned they used Beagles
in Iraq to test chemicals,
he put his head down on the rug and sobbed.
I shared his salinity; the unbearable thought
of abusing any living thing!

My heartbeat, this dog, my Camelot at all times
steadfast and kind; never argues or picks a fight,
never chides or reminds me of past mistakes;
wild babies can flop on his back, strangers stop to nuzzle.
His love, his heart, his faith are part of me,
his solid bulk, impressive canine beauty, solid soul –
the perfect antidote to a world of dog-eat-dog mentality.
The perfect partner for a dissident woman's heart.

CHRISTMAS IN THE 1980s (1988)

There is still a Christmas tree
Here speaking in the cold
And dark of old Christmas and solitary flares
The door closed but unlocked
Goats tucked into the barn with sheep
Under a dark necklace that holds the eye
Frosted geranium leaves and mud
Painted by the fog in white strands
And all these mornings dark as winter underneath
The old, cold December
Praise and deceit for families to remember
What they are after candles and the wreath
Each year the same dim star
Confusion and separation
The harm in what we are disrupt the theme
And make the message incomplete

RAINY NIGHT ON AN ENGLISH FARM (1989)

Asia, Donna, Leanne – these children
tangled around a coal fire, potato soup, the Sussex night;
young oracles madly driven by laughter,
then tears better fit for wide-open afternoons
filled with shining sun and space.
Instead, darkness that knows us all
drops on the indifferent sheep
the naked wood
the reservoir –
our loud and vocal heap,
this green plot
this necessary solitude.
Donna and Leanne stop to think;
their grandfather dying, to his woe.
Only sixty and already he is old,
fading like rain into the earth, maybe rising
in the spring with daffodils.
We all feed now beside this sodden farm;
the kindly wetness makes our arms
lean toward each other's hearts.
The things we need and long for
in this still and sometimes lonely place
are laughed about
and swallowed with our soup and bread.

YOUR MIND IS SOMEWHERE ELSE (1990)
(To Kenneth)

Please, come back. Stay rooted here
in this soil of our talk.
This idea you planted in me
I will tend because it is good seed.
You plough too many new fields,
cross-cutting your purposes,
rice in with the wheat;
stalks tangling, buds strangling.
We have not gathered a single
harvest together or beat the clods
off a single full-grown root.
I hoe, weed, water; serious in the task,
believing you will see the thing complete.
But we meet like strangers in the field
and I find you but a husk for this deed,
hardly conscious of how we will proceed.
The other half of you has moved
on to a new crop you've already flogged
to a buyer; like selling my legs
without a single attachment to your feet.

COFFEE WITH MY LOVER (1991)

My nose woke in your back
The smell of coffee drifting through rain
Rumpled bedding and hair
Sweet heavy air sliding its tongue through this eager door
To lick faces, our damp sex-aware bodies
A warm mother showering her perfume
Into the whispers of pre-dawn
When it is all clinging, slow waking
Skin yawns, two rooms merging, oh this clasp
Like milk and the moon slipping away
Secrets soft behind our closed eyes
Your breath like a baby too young for coffee
Tender this grey hour after night
Before action flows, before full sun
The hot brown river aroma of coffee welling
Across pillows bunched around us
Content with this abundance of comfort and repose
It is luxury to half-sleep
While our bellies breathe their duet
And our feet become grounded for waking
At the same lingering speed

JUST YOUR NORMAL CONFUSION (1992)

Oh, bedlam at home! The world moves in on me
even where I sleep and think and try to be human.
I shout, threaten, and blow my nose.
I should go to a meeting at 7:00. The dog
jumps over the fence, a flying lunatic
riveting me with his eyes – may be come too?
While my potato bakes in the microwave
(that strange machine, beeping and lights)
some plane overhead photographing my house
thinks I can pay for the picture and a new clutch
for the car. And she talks to me, this daughter
without a single stop sign in her vocabulary
and hair like haystacks surrounding her baseball cap;
all of them talking, talking at once,
cats snapping the heads off petunias,
peacocks parading around like look-at-me mannequins . . .
Leave me, everyone! while I touch this letter
on my bed, from Russia and some part of him,
so sure of his doubts, he believes them
and doesn't trust me, yet hangs on
like Spiderman linked to a fly by one sticky strand.
I just realized, this meeting will be over if I wait
for the potato and my perspective
to synchronise in my stomach, or my head
mixes up the signals and believes love
was meant to last for cats and peacocks and children,
potatoes, petunias and ideas
but maybe not for men who stay away so long
you can't remember how it sounded
when they said I love you
or if they said it at all.

AM I MY FATHER? (1993)

Every stone in my box, including frogs –
is that him ? I love roads that roll over hills,
like a voice calling, as he does.
Am I still his baby, crawling toward myself?
Did he give me brown eyes so I won't forget him,
conscience, so I would be his voice?
I hear the echo of my father even in my dog –
the things I choose and stand for,
suggesting him, that Samaritan, in my faith
derived from the beginning, my childhood,
when my father gave life a body
and passed me to the tempest, the song.

LOST FOOTING ON A SUNDAY AFTERNOON (1993)

I scratch mosquito bites sprinkled over my ribs
my blind skin softening in the wind off the oaks
I feel the light whisper into the kitchen
where I sit confused, wondering at misery on a day so fine
Should I cook dinner now or mow the lawn
or lie down in the shadows and be innocent?
Who flew in those balloons drifting through haze at 7:00 am?
She asks me, my daughter, how I amused myself as a child
and I can't explain. You can't guarantee imagination
but if it's catching, you do your own thing and reject insurance
as a protector of the failed dream.
There are moments like this, odd chromosomes
sucked from misshapen bones; nothing works, nothing happens
nothing fits and the sun slides down empty without thanks.
I am left with spaghetti, frustrated ambitions, remorse
for not being truthful when she asked what I did.
It's quite perfect really, depending on attitude
attitude I tell her is everything. But even now I can't swing it
like I should. Maybe it's something cosmic or arcane
not meant to be understood
These odd moments coupled with longing and silent tears
don't amuse me as I know they could some other time
when I'm stronger, set in a different orbit, properly defined
It is baffling to look out at the world with glory passing
and be cut off from it like a polar bear during a heat wave
in the London zoo. Sad until the weather changes
I never guessed being human would cause so much trouble
would tear the earth from its moorings
would render me speechless
would allow consciousness to act like a disease

WARM SUMMER NIGHT (1993)

My windows open to everything
I ever dreamed of in the way of hush and warm
bosom of earth filled with starlight and dry grasses
standing together in the papery perfume of summer
And the long slow rasp of crickets filling the pockets
of night with patient love. The fig tree breathes
through the green noses of tiny figs
The fern's spores tug at their moorings
then fall like dust upon the backs
of soft, plodding frogs whose legs ache for rain.
There is a oneness filtering through my screen
and including me if I pay attention and listen and imagine
my world within that world – fiddling, strumming, gliding
through the thick, sweet languor lying between
the August moons

COULD THIS BE EWE? (1993)

I've kissed Ewedora goodnight.
Don't ever say she's just a sheep with molars
for grinding grass and lips to cover them.
Her lips kiss me back.
She adores me at dusk
when I massage her neck where the bell rests.
She spreads her sheepness in the manure pile
in her way; alone, individually,
keeping her distance from the flock
as though she were a bell weather
or a seer or just an above-average sheep.
Am I an above-average human to love her
and the smell of her as I do?
Like a lanolin blanket infused with the character
of all the land around – the ferns
and coyote brush and bays,
the oaks and eucalyptus.
Things that live here as she does
and I do and we all do every day together,
moving in a single responsive ripple
with the fog, heat, wind, alarms, hawks.
But each night I am there for her
and she is waiting and I realise over and over
how much I love her.

TIME OUT WITH CHICKENS (1994)

Melting in the sun with the chickens clucking
pecking at corn, trimming the spiralled claws
of an old blind bantam hen, blackberry vines trailing
into the yard like green filaments of spiders

Cool shadows becoming warm, straw clinging close to my heart
I delay on the ledge leading into the barn
frantic to disarm myself here in the mysterious simplicity of hens
dropping eggs into nests, this soft feathered place
filled with heartbeat and clan, this easy shade
and chicken shit and easy mess

I want to sit here beyond sitting until I am unhurriedly
moving like light indiscernibly shifting by degrees
woven into clucking, hen voices and duck quack
until I nearly sleep and have no more need to hustle
in some deformed non-instinctual human way

When this happens in my day
when I have need to bide with hens and sit
with their slow fretless chicken needs, I know the time
has come for respite because I am weary
of the manic trivialness of big-brained calls to manage
everything and be everywhere and more calibrated
and relentless than the one soulful animal residing within
my chaos can ever wholeheartedly accept

FAREWELL, DEAR EWEDORA (1994)

I was too secure. So a pair of dogs robbed me.
I wouldn't have thought that in one night, with them barking
and me searching for my nine sheep with a flashlight
under the stars in my bathrobe, the patterns and loveliness
of ten years spent in the wild grass and coyote brush
with their great thick well-oiled coats wandering
through the green and gold seasons with their bells
reacting in syncopation with the baaing and bleating,
the whole linked rhyme of shearing and feeding
and lanolin-soft embraces at the end of the day with my Ewedora;
that old measured and treasured wool-covered woman
with her bent leg – that I could be turned so readily to grief

She lived her ten years, matriarch of this small flock
and as if it were a love affair, I found my own reflections in her.
I know we cared for each other, and she trusted me.
I lived with the pitch of her bell and knowledge of why they followed her
the way I wanted to through the brush, wild iris and ferns,
to where she sometimes napped under a stray old apple tree.

When I heard the barking and the sheep bells clanging,
I ran frightened, my heart thumping, grabbed the flashlight to go
and look. There was nothing. Just beautiful owls and moonlight,
plants breathing up out of the soil like always, and the place silent
with slumber as it's meant to be. But they'd already slain her;
that's what the barking meant. She was only a short way down the hill,
having faltered on that stiff leg and too old to run ahead of their teeth,
still too much of a sheep to defend herself or stand up to them
as I could have done. So they ripped apart her ears and her nose,
tore the fleece off her ribs, gnawed away her legs and rump,
reduced her to the pulp of a predator's manic joy . . .

Their owners were the real killers, turning dogs into accomplices
of the whole careless thing. When those dogs are captured,
there'll be deep regret, but did those men learn anything?

At first, I looked for her everywhere, hoped she was just missing.
Then finally I knew, coming up the trail where I smelled death,
and found the deep pity of her wasted under the brush,
decaying and no longer my dear old Ewedora –
except for the bell, touching the soul of her stolen being.

MY GIRL HAS ADD (1994)

I coax her – she doesn't come.
I open my arms, I reach to touch her arm,
enfold her, smell that flower of her cheek,
but she doesn't want me near.
I lose her in the labyrinth of non sequiturs,
an incessant barrage from the mouths of misguided synapses.
Mom, I saw a flying saucer! Just kidding.
My game has been cancelled. Not really.
I grab her shadow. I want to scream.
She took a dollar from my purse.
She threw her lunch in the garbage.
She looks deep into my eyes
and deliberately forgets to tell the truth.

Where do I turn for courage,
living as I do in this small house with non-cooperation,
egg on the floor, her unruly hair?
I'm alone, unsupported, worried
that she's only twelve, though budded.
Pre-adolescence; they're designed that way.
But others don't realise you have to stay with it
night and day to experience how it wears you down,
renders you shocked at your own outbursts.
Wasn't I once patient, tolerant, unusually kind
to animals? But she rips off
my appearance, throws in a reality
I never bargained for, until guilt
devours me once more when the curve
of her young face glistens with our tears.

WHEN THE FAMILY GETS TOGETHER (1994)

I want to hide;
they come on like an Armada
a barnacle-ridden flotilla
with so much flotsam in tow
I can only handle them one by one

Give me the wine glass, the refuge,
the bosom of my own living room
out of harm's way

I do love them
but we never learned to step aside
for the common good;
almost, but not quite strong enough
to laugh at this tangled rigging,
our shifting cargo below deck.
We talk the talk of the intellect
but each big wave scatters us
and we storm off nursing our shipwrecks
in mysterious harbours
where no other can drop anchor

We sail under the same flag
but loyalty ends there;
we are actually separate nations
guided by separate laws.
When we assert them, there is sabotage;
something always founders on rocks
that rip out the bottom
of our fidelity to a family course

My soul floats
in a life raft of lights, music;
steering away until I no longer hear
the waves beating
their hearts out on the crumbling reef

(Camelot came from America in a crate, spent six lonely months in English quarantine, and after six sublime months together with me in Somerset, succumbed to the insidious effect quarantine had filled him with, and died. Losing him was the worst trauma I've ever suffered in my whole life.)

MAGNIFICENT DOG (1995)

I want to do him justice, be entirely focused
on every large ounce of him lying black-coated
in shade, jowls mopping up unsullied dust.
If I move beyond his half-conscious range
he will pull to his feet and follow wherever I go
as if my life and his were one four-legged intent
to be together, as though even the ozone of myself
must include him when he's shut behind the fence.

He hovers outside the back window
observing my being denied him inside;
then one clear bark to remind me he is there,
to reinforce the chemistry that so obviously
describes all the countless ways we are linked,
even in his eyes following to embrace me
when we go to our separate beds for the night.

Then, before closing, I hunch close,
breathe in the smooth dense fur of his cheek,
stroke the loyal, dependable black casing and know
exactly what he is thinking, like me, juggling
with whether we are both more human or dog.

MY BROTHER COMES ON THE RAIN (1995)

This rain came straight from Hawaii
heavy with passion fruit and vines
the warm thick smell of ferns, pandanus,
volcano mulch, the vapour of lacy waterfalls
and hibiscus, the lushly humid hint of time
immemorially mysterious and fecund green

My brother breathes this every day
his living a continuous perfume.
I wonder if this process of tropical earth
in the making affects the way he dreams
and thinks; so rich and succulent an atmosphere
constantly flowering, erupting in juice
and steam, pineapple, ash and sand
and curls of streaky foam lining the blue sea's
boundary line for whales, all the things
I can't name because they are intertwined
and incidentally came in on the rain
that brought me close to him.

MARRIAGE, WITH CATS (1996)

When we were married we acquired cats.
I brought home strays, young mothers.
We raised a family; not children, just cats.
Then we moved across the country by car
and took them all with us, where understandably
throughout the night they climbed drapes in motel rooms.
When we set up house again in California
they did too, and lost a few lives in the process.
Strange things happen when you inhabit
a semi-wilderness; bobcats and fanged flying things,
disorienting fog, forests hiding bears and mountain lions.
We weathered most jolts, up to a point –
then came divorce. You went, I stayed and the cats
remained with me and once you were gone,
you never asked anything about them again.
They were my cats, not yours.
In fact, all the time we were together they were
my cats. I fed them, took them to the vet for shots,
until they got old, like you, and one by one they died;
tumours, infirmity, the scourge of years;
Tricot went into convulsions when her ears sickened.
Midnight was sewn up after exploratory surgery
and came home stiff and sightless in a box.
And the others, Aphro and Starlight
went through their own pain and put me through mine,
but you never asked about them, never fondled them again.
When I told you Tarzan was dying, that last bony man
of a cat who slept all day in a box stinking
of incontinence and rot,
you couldn't walk a few steps into the kitchen
even to look at him and say a last goodbye.
You only said he's old, and left it at that.
The sum total of your affection.
He wasn't part of your heart; your life maybe

like a token, nothing more. Just like you were never
really part of my heart; just a construct of married life
based on convenience and that was the basic gist of it.
I loved living with those cats, but I could never live
again with you, or any man who doesn't feel the way I do.

THE PARTS OF OUR WHOLE (1996)

Your cat is also your life.
He has been part of you
in your kitchen, your closet,
peeing on your parked shoes
sleeping on your belly or hip.

When he grows old and forgetful
and is a ragged, bony thing with stripes
you know it's even more than that.
He's the hammock you've slept in
the keeper of moles
your laughter, your frown
the soft feline adroit body you've danced with
for so many years
like a special person
the grandfather you show to a chair
so he can doze
and after, together
you can do anything

MY DAUGHTER CHICKEN-SITS (1996)

I'm not trying to be funny and it's not what you think.
She's noble, heroic. She sits on the dry grass inside the yard
reading Catcher in the Rye at 6:30 on a Sunday night.
Fog is rolling in and she and the dog are both inside the fence
that holds in the hens and ducks and for the most part
keeps out bobcats, raccoons, foxes, coyotes;
the native inhabitants of these compromised California hills.

Without a good book, she'd quibble. If her friends could see
what she is doing, she'd probably be the object of ridicule.
But she goes at my urging without needing to be pushed.
I promise it's worthy to experience the end of day
away from the input of humans, to just sit there with the others,
be one of them for a few pages, the sifting changes passing over
carrying a great rapture she had no idea of before.

She may get it, she may not.
But this is different from the usual teenage trial and error.
I want her to sense something down there in the chicken shit
and stickers, the light changing into wet molecules,
ducks and hens talking in another language . . .
something she may remember when walls close her in
and her thirst for inspiration makes guarding chickens
a thing of value, not just some futile, bizarre, wasted exercise.

PLANTED A TREE, BURIED A CAT (1996 – tribute to Tricot)

I didn't expect it so suddenly; after 18 years
of spending life together, to take this small cat
to the doctor for a bad ear and drive home with her
empty beside me. She died in my lap with a tiny mew,
eyes already glassy – where do the pupils go?

It isn't so much death and its awful finality;
it's about familiarity and what you come to expect
in the way of routine: her voice, fur like teased hair,
her manner of spreading on a thigh and drooling
and always looking for a new place to hide for sleep
and leaving it dusted over with the residue of her coat.

She's in the cold March earth now stiff in a box
with jonquils nodding to her deep departure
beside the gravenstein apple tree my mother gave me
for planting, unknowingly joining with her body
whose most slender bones, like branches of my new tree,
will be sought out and married beneath spring grass.

Though I say these things, and she's only a cat, I can't
help but think about death and how it happens; her suffering
for an hour, being poked and measured the way vets do,
unless you demand they stop and let death arrive naturally.

Now everything is strange, final, and about love;
which fully absorbed me when I walked out of there
carrying the limpness of her near-finality – more real
than professionally listening for a heartbeat and trying
to explain what to do, when only instinct listens.

She is here with me now, organising my memory –
a small cat sitting on the kitchen floor asking for dinner.
I wish so much I could have her home, warm-blooded.

THIS GIRL (1997)

A cold rip in the air
leads me to slippers.
She, the teenager, voice of unreason,
wasn't overheated before
but suddenly, around 9:00 pm
the breeze pouring through her window
whips my hair.
She has no knowledge of what I've said
or even of her own body.
There is silence in her loft,
the temperature and me climbing together
to see if she still breathes.
She complains about gates and buttons,
loyalty, our dog – but will she sleep.

Her young body is distorted
as though wishful thinking
had devoured its pre-adulthood,
as though she gave up
what she couldn't afford to lose
to a local cult;
not just another abductor
but all of us, every day of the week
offering something light-hearted;
if we'd just take pity and slip away
with something she doesn't value
and would never miss,
perhaps we could help free her
to learn more about who she really is.

WHAT IS POSSIBLE (1997)

What kind of father would take his child to see Scream?
All those decapitations
And he does it behind my back, knowing I'd react
but his peculiar indifference allows it
and what can I do when we live one hundred miles apart?
If Picasso asked you to marry him
would you say no because of the wrinkles around his eyes?
What of younger men and older women –
what keeps them apart? They have coffee, but beyond that
is there anything significant? Do the tables turn?
Would you deny a great mind in a ruined body?
And one's mother, never moving from her chosen position;
never rethinking or growing past her juvenile embolism,
an identifiable old mantra that reappears year after year.
And there are teenage daughters who never trust you
no matter what you do for them or how you answer. . .
We danced in the rain the other night, she and I.
I called her bluff. She said let's do it and we did
and she never expected that.
But there's more to come.
She must be filled with insecurity to put so many others down.
And there we have it late in January when that rain
fills our yearnings with mud and slime.
This is a difficult time of counting months;
hatreds fester, sheep die in the flooding of liquid
overkill. It is a time to wonder
who or what is important, and depending, why bother
going out on a limb for such small tokens of empowerment.

NO REMORSE (1997)

That she would give away
so much for so little in return –
a phone call to a friend
is worth a hundred lies

She is inside grandma's house unseen
and then she dials
and all the while her eyes are on the door
lest an anxious mother should appear
'How dare you sneak away and hide!'

I heard you bang the table with the phone
and when I looked, you'd disappeared –
hidden in a closet so later you could claim
the bus was late and you'd had to stop to pee
at grandma's house

At first she disavowed the whole thing
I was coming up the hill and saw you leave
I left a message on your phone.
But it wasn't what she said
Everything was made up; fabrications
laced with intrigue that would wow the CIA

I never can believe her now;
for a temporary score, she betrays my trust.
How you see yourself is how we see you too, I say
but maybe we were all that way;
devious little shits who lied
and made their lives a joke
until they came of age.

MY CAMELOT (1998)

He's a dog with mettle, even a nose for nettles.
He barks inside the house but never
raises his voice unnecessarily;
a series of wrummps to call for his pillow bed.
I sniff his cheek while he cradles his head
in my armpit, so calm and gentle a black saint,
an exemplary water lily on the vast pond of life.
But give him a rawhide chew for something to do
and relieve boredom, he'll sit up and vote,
as though this small thing was about managing a kingdom.

We have intimate discussions about unpaved roads
and pig's ears, leg lifts, walking in rain,
people's treatment of their unloved dogs (he doesn't want
to hear that); when I mentioned they used Beagles
in Iraq to test chemicals,
he put his head down on the rug and sobbed.
I shared his salinity; the unbearable thought
of abusing any living thing!

My heartbeat, this dog, my Camelot at all times
steadfast and kind; never argues or picks a fight,
never chides or reminds me of past mistakes;
wild babies can flop on his back, strangers stop to nuzzle.
His love, his heart, his faith are part of me,
his solid bulk, impressive canine beauty, solid soul –
the perfect antidote to a world of dog-eat-dog mentality.
The perfect partner for a dissident woman's heart.

MY SELF-EFFACING CHILD (1998)

You come home and two police cars are parked in the drive
and it so happens your 16 year daughter is sitting in one
hands cuffed behind her back, and the wind suddenly feels very cold.
She talked about committing suicide, took the old butcher knife
from its sheath and made pin lines on her arms,
sobbing, said the friend with her on the phone, wild with grief
for love of the girl the parents will no longer let her see.
She's at the hospital nearby being tested for drugs, a routine thing
and they're all very kind. What do you do now after dark
not knowing how to curb the flood of doubt and fear
for a girl who lives in a vast land thronged with guns
and children who kill themselves and also rape other lives?

Can we leave them alone? Where must she turn to know herself?
Do you take all the kitchen knives and the aspirin and the bleach
out of the house on every errand? When they lie,
do you take away phone privileges, their radio, the keys?
Do cries for help equate with calls for guns? Is that how it is now?
She'll stay somewhere else tonight to be quiet and think.
But if kids with broken hearts turn to suicide as balm
where does that leave the parents and the way we communicate?
You wait at home alone, mystified, aching,
a small boat on the turbulent sea of mixed messages,
useless stratagems, anger that basic emotions
could so easily lead into deadly minefields –
where before, in ignorance, you laughed and coped.

WHAT DOES SHE MEAN WHEN SHE SAYS SOMETHING DIFFERENT? (1999)

This girl of mine looks me in the eye like two brown rivets
swears no, she didn't do it, those scissors must be lying
on my bed, but they're not
so she must be – not on my bed
but the other reclining word
because I've had those scissors 25 years and they haven't
walked away yet

Young and pretty, white teeth and a clicky tongue
her buns like brown cupcakes, the icing to come
lush child of India like a palace
of contradictions
She took bread and bananas and honey and pecans
and forgot them behind her books
deliberately without consideration
until the little fruit flies came and revealed the trick

She once went down the road and disappeared
into her grandmother's house
walked back out to her fears when out backs were turned
to talk about suicide on the phone to a bunch of girls
Oh, the terrible things she did,
like a cub with a halo around her head
and no remorse

ROSIE POSY CHRISTMAS (1999)

How do your fern-lines grow?
You in your caravan draped by the vines
and a radical wine
the river flows on by your toes
and rows upon rows of Rosemary knows
are draped in the foggiest trees.
She may sneeze and may sneeze and fall on her knees
but she will never quite go with the flow.
Oh Guerneville is blest that there is her nest
on the banks of the bold Russian river.
But though she may quiver and beg for redress
she will never not ever give in
or thoroughly pine
for she will certainly not be an Indian-giver.
Warm may her walls sit and cat all a-purr.
the winkle and wankle of life in the spackle
quite enough to inure her forever, as blessed,
and most fully equipped to live in the thick
and the ready awhile of the smile
of life on this mysterious river,
a maiden so quick with her wit and her wile
you can spot her from miles afar.
For now as this century hastens to close
and quite possibly marries this loveliest rose
as she rows up the stream and looks to the west
for the rest of the best way to smile.
Oh sister, my love, may you wear the above
with your wit and a great dazzling flash of your style.

FAMILY TREE (1999)

I want to go into history
the hereafter
beyond
my next life
the spirit life

with animals.
a cat, a dog
chickens
a few sheep

juicy and wet together
in the way of things alive
unlike deserts or Mars

cow's face in the sweet peas
lambness all over spring
equal in the higher sense
as partners
the way we get on

I feel them
every time we meet
saying aren't we just something
together
and wouldn't it be awful
if we weren't

HAS SHE REALLY GONE FOR GOOD? (2000)

Blue tack stuck on my daughter's walls
Millions of pieces that take off the wall paper of this rented house
Whatever I do, however I feel, whatever happens in the world
The A38 roars on and on like a pile driver, a souped up nerve
The world's juggernauts ripping through Somerset

I've seen a red deer in the forest
Standing motionless, watching me watch it
Then I drove past Watchet looking for a place to live
Like a deer searching out it's own piece of forest
Like a mind sitting at a desk watching Wales glow
Late in the afternoon when the rain has stopped
And that's no answer, there's no call, no place there, nothing

It is a weird time after she has left,
Gone to California and never coming back
All the junk I stuff in the car and drive off with
Like taking home lost dogs, bringing in near-death cats
Like the dark highways I cruise in my sleep
Her paper, her hated pajamas, the stuff under her bed
Back to the blue tack on her walls, the mention
About killing herself so she wouldn't ever have to live in England

This August twilight glows, perfumed with water
Flower baskets heavy in themselves
Statements of respectability, more persuasive than family
Who merely sit without flowers on the fence.
A hard time for me and the others of us involved
In these diatribes about who's right and how it should be

While it keeps raining here, washing it away
The cerebral cleansing of mastery
The sheep baaing together, trees leaning, grass
Intertwining, the horseback riders still riding, Wales
Sitting across the channel like a glowing crown
My amazement that we have to argue at all.

LIKE NONE OTHER (2000)

He climbs the stairs to me like a pup seeking its mother
limping up each tread thumpingly, dragging his bad leg
which he swings around the door jamb, then coming to rest
on the sheepskin rug beside my bed.
His stomach gurgles like a river bumping over dumped refrigerators
he smells like a wild hyena, a smouldering mound of fur
a warm dark hairy smell like a grandfather, a summer ditch
and he carries it up the stairs one step at a time
my great magnificent boy now so unjustifiably deformed
cells leaping over each other in self-perfecting destruction;
what they call soft tissue sarcoma, malignant in any terms
that odious description of slowly decaying life;
how I despair at it coming inexplicably before his time
so that he doesn't eat and we can't walk together
and everything is crushed and strange
as though we were being divided by an insanely jealous idiot

I know him so well – he grew up in my skin
We were one body; I had only to flick my chin and he went
He laughed when I tickled his nose
I sneezed when he tickled mine or maybe it was the reverse
Whatever he did or said was my copy
as though we thought with one brain, like twins
and our hearts beat together in everything we did

I measure his nobleness and there's no end to it;
imagine a great glorious black mixture of dog
that has never once been stupid or bad and in the best
dog way never complained or fussed.
Such a superb character, so much better than most friends.
Which makes it worse around the end, the paragon of him
becoming an old, cold, dead dog whose own eyes
have lost their sight of me; his tail lies still, teeth silent.
I kiss him and weep over his shining body and nothing happens;

he has gone far beyond and his flesh lies motionless on the ground
or in my bedroom or the back of the car or on a cold slab
and he's nothing except the dense flares of memory
that swim majestically around his final inertness.
It's the saddest thing; it's beyond sadness. It's grief
without boundaries. Never have I felt so desolate and numb.

WE THREE (2001)

Ah yes, my mother's cane hanging over the chair
Asia with her cropped red hair
Cat on the Welsh plaid blanket
Dog on his hairy bed
The cold, cold night wrapping its fist around our breath

How many lights are settled on this little tree
How many pilchards did we eat
Why did my bread crumble and what did we do for heat
When the oil tank went dry?

Asia with her CD player and pink nightie
Mum who washes dishes and peels apples for sauce
How we heroically surge forward, then fall back
May be a prescription for most families
And the subtle and outrageous ways they cope

Carols, coal, milk, tea, blankets, this home's litter,
Who's using an excess of toilet paper,
What would you like to do while here, I ask
And no one answers. The cat comes home alive

Asia likes to tease; puts dog hair on Grandma's coat,
Strums her little guitar and watches Dawson's Creek.
What a difficult family we are!
Even on the summit of Dunkery and in the combes
As though a spur to cooperate had been misplaced.
And yet how lovely too, precious and different
During this unexpected Christmas in Porlock, this big event,
The coming together of mother, grandmother, 'child'
A trilogy for love and teamwork's sake.

(My sister Rosemary has 'terminal' lung cancer. Two years younger than me; a tall, willowy, blue-eyed blonde with above-average intelligence, excellent singing voice, artistic and linguistic skills, acting ability, a poet; not everyone's cup of tea, but something for everyone. By mid-December she was gone.)

SHE CAN'T TAKE IT ANY MORE (2002)

So you've smoked nearly your whole life
but we endure such things and live on,
this family connected to Uncle Albert's stalk,
a shrivelled 105 when he went belly up in his flowers

Now all day a lump in my throat
because of this particular someone in the family dying;
a joke maybe, a misprint, that huge fog in her lungs
not just nicotine debris, but pneumonia
and if she survived that, and walked out for coffee again,
and carried on chatting with Lefty her cat,
made plans and choices and did Tai Chi and yoga,
how could she be on the way out?
Lock her door, pull down the curtain, pills on the table, crawl under
the bedding?
Dwelling on this makes me feel I am also dying

The pair who invented us pushing ninety;
remembering the fishlet they made together,
recoiling now to think of her floating before them down the stream;
I pity them having to carry this sorrow like a coffin

The heavier since it is her Mother who will convert Rosemary
into ash-form, with commentary, and install her on family land
to link with the dead sheep, chickens, lost dogs we knew;
offer her bad lungs and habits to the familiar earth
to combine with ferns and coyote brush drifting around them

Lavishing her lengthy fair cleverness
on a philosophical tree sprouting overhead
to make us recall how she could sing and dance and paint;
eliciting in me a gentle envy and the wish I'd known
her sloe-eyed French speaking Serbian husband
in Beograde for an inkling of why she fell apart on divorce
and after, never got put back together

One of her big canvases watches me from a wall,
poems in folders, letters with a unique tone;
the particularness of her scrawl and its inverted wisdom,
coffee habits and rolled cigarettes, the breathlessness,
ironic snort, the way she walked out of movies, hee-haw laughter

Rosemary ended in this last resort by the river;
talked to her lost teenage daughter, said farewell to Father,
breathed oxygen, did coffee, still smoked, regaled her friends;
like Seneca and Plato – our stoic non-conformist
jesting among us, whispering fables,
playing her flute in the moonlight at 2:00 am,
long hair forming a versatile shield around her memory.

(5 days after I wrote this, she was dead. Rosemary left on the evening of December 15, 2002)

STOLEN SIBLING (2002)

My little sestra she called me
then turned off

I wanted to hear her voice on the phone
Somerset to California
my stone walls, her caravan
on the Russian River

I'm not feeling well she said, not to me
but to the air around the phone
held by a carer

I never talked to her again.
My mother tried the locked door, looked
through the window
and there was my sister lying dead
in her bed, pill bottles
scattered around

Christmas was one of the worst of my life;
I must have been grieving, because I stayed
home, all on my own
wondering about the meaning
of things, how death
takes away the givers of presents,
the very heart
of those you belong to

MOTHERING SUNDAY (2002)

Full-blooming light
pressed through each window,
the soothing cadence of a horse clopped by,
uniting us in the basic experience of sun

So that suddenly
I wanted to be an upheaval of joy
and jig up and down in the lane
with someone wise and eternal
—like my mother,
and exclaim over the first topic on our lips:
each other, how she came first,
then brought me along
so we'd be here one Sunday
arms filled with flowers
and a celebration of mothers

I wanted to be dizzy together
in laughter and words,
walk together and eat
as though we were girls
who had been blind all year
and mindless but for one single thing;
to gulp down the sun
and gather it in like dry laundry
just before rain

MOST BLESSED FRIEND (2002)

All of a sudden, with the sun still shining, my dinner
cooking in the wok, an ear tuned
to tourists squawking, the rumblings
and smell of other dinners, the way evening
in a small tourist village draws not quite evenly together

I felt Camelot my dog moving invisibly
toward me as if he were a shadow on paws,
his fur like night, clean and dark
eyes gleaming with love and forgiving

As though the ordeal of quarantine
after we came here, together but apart, he bearing
the brunt, will be a cage for the rest of my life
and his ashes a reminder of what we both lost

Six months of separation,
then six months downhill and dying and me
living, but dying after him in my whole being,
grief falling on my forsaken skin, my palms
reaching down and stroking his unmoving feet,
the way he tells me about wandering dejectedly in his sleep
during all that time we couldn't be together.

So I wept profoundly, knowing he was talking to me,
some deep connection,
the satin ears I'd often caressed and the fine wisdom
I'd written about for others read,
the insult of misery at the end; a theft
of inhuman and dog-minded proportions

I cannot begin to tell you what I had forsaken
in the upheaval to relocate to Britain
and how I couldn't relive this, bitter and aching,
without some raw form of his presence
circling around me, a warm sense of reunion and love

In the far atmosphere, a bone clicking
the great transcription where shared language
is licked clean and finalised, passed along
through two open wounds melding
for one tumultuous and never-to-come-again shared moment

AFTER MY MOTHER GOES HOME (2002)

She's on a plane now, the difficult one
and how I miss her
hummed through the sky
drooping over a tray of fake food
yet eating every fake crumb

Cars move, wind blows, the village temporises
to some extent, as though my mother
had never been back-bent along the lane
and necklace of Porlock village shops
that eventually led her home

Mother, up there between the plane's wings!
Do you walk the aisles
without your cane?

I want you to know, tonight I sigh.
It makes me feel lonely not to see your room's light
showing beneath the door.

This isn't what I'd planned to write;
the essence, the suggestion skipped away
when the phone rang and I lost the bigger point.
But still. . .

I know better now who you are and how
the small faint scales of you, the occasional roar
dropping like heavy liniment into my old sores
has both wounded me and healed

I won't forget how were here in my place
like a flame-spouting dinosaur,
Hildegard von Bingen sagely speaking,
the worth of you softly hidden like fleece already woven
into its own unique style and form.
Your smile rising from the concealed spring of Life.

EVEN AS SMALL AS THIS (2002)

My mother stood washing dishes;
Later I'll wash my pink flannel nightgown she explained.
I'll always remember her rounded back
At the sink scrubbing a pot

The small notes, tiny flourishes
Something that crops up unexpectedly
The way she told stories about her youth
The awesome older brother
The voice without emotion as though scabs and halos
had turned to dust

Her litanies about Sierra Leone, Delhi, Milano
Past exultations
The coriander on her lip
Bananas and peanuts by the sea

I ache for her to combine past and present
To write a book that reveals what's buried
To be here now flourishing
To speak up despite the riddles
Still controlling all her dreams

I WAIT FOR YOU (2003)

I'm writing these words
but my eyes are weeping – I can hardly see.

Three years on, more?, I cry for him, my Camelot.
My dog. Not just because I miss him, knowing
he could still be here with me, but how
he died, the clumsiness of it, the lack, the loss,
the sorrying ride I got, his life denied

The lapses, from California home to cage
on plane to cage in van to cage in kennelled Somerset;
cage on cage on cage! The death of him, confined

The bones I brought, my visits, sad eyes, loss of weight,
stupidity of running around inside the wire
where once we'd loped across the land
and talked and shared and lived as one, the dog-built me

Quarantine: I'd come inside his little door; he sat aloof
with hopeless eyes. For half a year, those stupid months,
I never saw him smile. A gull without a tide
his killer world within those walls
the settling dust that kills, instils its sense of hopelessness,
the dog thought: *Here I am, confined*
shut in, held back, denied, my human love withheld,
my weakened legs, dismantled bark, extinguished spark; Her,
the one with whom I understand my Dog
has gone, she seldom reappears, I'm lost, I sink
The freedom I'm allowed won't slow my death; I know
her grief will follow me, and weep and weep and weep . . .

THESE TWO ARE MINE (2003)

The phone is going to ring
and a voice, maybe Mary's, will tell me
my father has passed on

This is the pain I hold in my hand
while drinking my tea
the fog that drowns my feet while walking

That message I have to confront
the private war in my heart
however fine all the hours of daylight and no rain

He will have vanished without our talking
one last time.
Our issues clouded
travelling with me like a box of old papers
rubber bands and paper clips
affecting the way I move on

Or the ringing phone
could be about my mother
who may have clandestinely worked her bone-twisted body
into the front seat of her car
behind the driver's wheel
and driven off to her final confrontation

Or she has collided with the door jamb
and dropped a handful of plates
as she sloped to the floor

Having them empty out my life
is like touching family history page by page
setting a match to it
hovering bleakly on the margins while it slowly burns

THAT DEEP WOMAN (2003)

Oh lordy, I had just navigated all the way
from my heart, down through my veins;
Grasmere to Porlock in my good, green car

Could I just drive?
No, I had to stop for a bit of bland coffee
and a lukewarm motorway chat with God

When I finally walked in the door of my house,
Rosemary was there waiting.
Her poems from America in an envelope on the floor.

I sat and ate a late dinner while thumbing through the pages
her picture with its laughing face watching me on the table
I felt all my held-back love and sat there and unexpectedly cried
as though re-entering my heart after driving over 300 miles
down the maimed shin bone of the world.

I came home to Rosemary and cried.
Rosemary, how I love you.
The way you handled everything, even what was most intense;
if need be, leaving for a cigarette and not coming back.

Now I hear you lifting yourself
with the pulleys of heaven and guffawing
in that little roped-off field
where you and the other artists are lying down
drinking, eating cheese, sharing a joint maybe,

Remembering us. Painting a cloth for the others;
Rosemary – waiting for me, your big sister
with a cup of real coffee so we can talk freely
and write poems together and add our fuel to the stars.

A DISPARATE PAIR (2003)

I want so much to talk to you
like your baby slug, your chrysalis
asking tell me, now what?

What do you mean dying? How could you
fall, old oak, your branches pressed everywhere

You went to Hungary and rescued refugees
as a Quaker, not your normal thing
so that entitles you to ten extra years

You're sick, miserable, You want to go?
I've never wanted that for you, not ever
You're my father—I'm not ready to release you yet

I sit here eating Thai Chilli crisps
drinking red wine. Rain pours down
Maybe you think I am strong, I can deal with this
One duck drowning in mud is all I need to go mad.

Or war in Iraq. The whole lot of them,
loose marbles, blood clots, stones in their veins
I cannot imagine how we've got it so wrong

Then my mother has a stroke
(a series of them, a speeded-up heartbeat they say)
and she too travelled the world:
Russia and China, the Red Sea
three years in Sierra Leone, India, Cuba—
just ask. Ask me, she isn't able to talk

Will I know who I am when you're both gone?
Who will have answers to the questions then;
who will take me under their wing?

MY FATHER'S 89TH BIRTHDAY (2003)

This is my gift to you.
My thoughts from my now to your now.
Dad with your hands in the oil
on the head gasket and the pistons
sometimes sitting in the kitchen late nights
with the greasy rag wiping off a cylinder.
Dad who led me by the hand
to the frogs and the stars and 'goodnight moon',
a dog somewhere in the background like a watchful child.

Dad of the far countries, coming home
with a Hungarian peasant blouse (which I still have).
Dad of the ice fields and fish, Denali and Sputnik,
our cross-country drive (you let me off in Idaho
or was it Oregon?) and your Alcan Highway
and the theft of Sputnik waiting in your car

You and those unexpected ducklings
and Laddie, the roamer, and Ireland
when you wouldn't stop for gas.
But you officiated at my wedding in the woods
during your days of mixed Grace.

Landlord Dad, Taft Avenue man
cooking late after you got home,
waking startled when your homebrew exploded
under the bed—I still wonder if you mopped it up
and returned it to the bottle and went back to sleep.

Birthday Dad, recovering from a long bout of flu
when you said you were ready to 'move on'.
But I'm not ready, so I knew it wasn't your time.
Otherwise, I wouldn't be remembering you as I do
all these years; your first puppy to appear, your first cricket.

A DAUGHTER DIES AND MAIMS THE MOTHER (2003)

We all hated losing Rosemary, naturally.
But the way she lived killed her
and she'd partly died in the mind much earlier
which is why my mother became a carer

Which is what she did for years;
soup, stew, carrots and lettuce from her garden
designed to nourish Rosemary

Movies, coffee, books, alternating lines of poetry
took her here, brought her this and that
worried, watched, carried;
years and years of doing that
regularly, on schedule, dutifully, with great intent

Then Rosemary died
during our mother's 86th year
After a broken collarbone, a crashed car
osteoporosis, forgetfulness, two canes
cataracts removed, a dislocated jaw
and pulses of life in Italy, Africa, India, Timbuktu

She fell apart when Rosemary left permanently.
Messy house, doesn't drink enough or eat
dirty cat bowl, lack of heat, in bed til 10:00 am

We scold. Be good, aware, wake up, we care.
It isn't that. Her light has gone, that focus
the regular appearance as a Needed One

So talk about her then, what do you remember?
Describe it all—where you went and when and how.
She sat there by the window in the old blue chair

Mother's voice grows soft; she needs to open up
about the girl who died, that daughter at her breast
the skinny one, blond, blue eyed, distant in her youth
and later lost, a temporary lack of soup
or what, we'll never know. Poor Mother crying
soundlessly, can't ask for help. The blue chair empty
the daughter turned to dust
and scattered just outside the door

(A deep emotional conflict; why am I vegetarian after having a mother able to kill animals?
And much more than that—why are we, both Quakers, so much at odds? Why were we
never able to talk to each other and resolve our differences?)

A WOMAN OF HER OWN (2004)

Why did she and cousin Bob in Glendale
slay dozens of pigeons together?
Why did Grandma Marmee look on
as though no such thing ever happened,
as though she stirred her voice into the gravy
and boiled it right out of her?

Why did my mother kill the ducks I cared for
and cook them and put them on the table
and cut the haunch off a freshly-slain deer?

Why did my sheep expire
only when I went to live in England
and they were entrusted to her care?
My sweet dog disappeared too
and the goats and the peacocks—
though she wouldn't have eaten them
or given them to somebody else to eat. . .
But it was as if no one had been left in charge

Why did things die when my mother
was the sole nurse, sentinel, custodian?
And why did this include my heart, my love for her,
Christmas, anything to do with family?

It was thought we were all wounded, left for dead,
and nobody came with remedies
or genuine life-saving equipment.
We just quietly, subtly stabbed each other;
no obvious wounds, nothing overt.

Nonetheless, in our own ways, we all bled to death.

MY MOTHER'S HANDS (2004)

Her thumbnail kept splitting.
She would show me in a way
that was almost an apology;
an inherited thing,
something her father had too.
She never mentioned
whether it was painful.
She had coarse hands, like a peasant
farmer's wife. Hands that would be good
at milking cows and strong
enough to pull big turnips
up by the roots.
They were hands that could lift
food-filled frying pans to the table
with a single sweep.
And yet, her handwriting
was controlled and small,
as though she were a teacher of penmanship.

I don't remember her hand
ever cupping my cheek.

HER LAST MOMENT (2004)

While the morning's final minute
still clung to you,
was there a black sky
squinting behind your fruit trees?
Did you hover in the centre of that minute
like a rabbit clutched in the stare
of an approaching wolf?
Did the light whisper to you with a shimmer
before you crumpled .
naked into the tub?
Could you feel your heartbeat
as the grains of your soul
limped out the bathroom window?
Was it anything like you'd imagined
when finally the sunlight faded
and you knew it had come for you
like a cloud picking up a leaf?

In that flash, did you assemble
your wholeness and the fact that it was Sunday
and the porcelain was cold under your feet?
Did you blaze for an instant
while remembering your life and your children?

Then God buzzed you,
called you to the heavenly phone, as it were,
and you answered.
I, your daughter, cannot even invent
the conversation, what you murmured
to yourself and all of us
when it snatched your heartbeat
and allowed blackness to enter your caverns
when it came time to go

UNEXPECTED EXIT (2004)

My mother was good at saving
and always set a little something by.
Lately I find in myself the same propensity
and wonder if she was the source.

She has just passed on, so I can never explore
that curve of being, our similarity of lobes,
the way our poles crashed in oceans of misunderstanding

The hardness now lies in facing
her utter silence – not just the natural hush of sleep
behind a closed door, but the way she has become
unreachable and far colder than she ever was in life.

This is the silent terminus, the line's end
for questions, probing, patching up and further testing,
She has entered the unfathomable tunnel of no return

I can't compose a letter and expect
a reply next month, a phone call on my birthday,
a little Christmas box, advice dressed up as point of view

The bone-thinned old body that collapsed naked
in the bath and lay chilling in a broth
of her own warm excrement and blood
will never skirt the truth with me again or scan
me with blue eyes, ambivalent inside her soft skin

Nor will her recountings of what she found
in India and China, West Africa, Milano, Timbuktu
have a chance once more to stir the summer air between us
as she heats my admiration with those wondrous excursions

I will not look again upon the bed she made so neatly
or stand unnoticed, watching as she labours
in her companionable garden or hear
how softly she spoke into the phone – it's all past
holding my arms around. I can only visit the crannies
of memory, reread the letters, lay out old photographs,
realign her within my hopes and losses and dreams

SHE WASN'T FINISHED WITH HER LIFE (2004)

I hear my mother growling in her ashes
her hump raised rebelliously
Why did you take me away? Put me back
in the bath to begin from where I left off;
you don't know how much more I still have to offer.
Her hump quivers and her hands clench
and I know that steely look in those blue eyes

She offers a bowl of cherries from her tree
I have to stand back to accept them
lest the stones take aim and maim me

I have to go home and rethink. Who is a mother,
just because she gives birth to some little
apparatus which then follows on, maybe shooting
rabbits or painting her toenails or having
a mental breakdown, does or doesn't absolve one
from what she has brought forth

Still, all those notebooks, those drawers filled
with paper, social conundrums that made her think,
I.F. Stone's Weekly cleansing the muddy waters.
She was still thinking, deciding, figuring out,
weighing, matching up one thing with another
when she inadvertently finished
naked in the bathroom; unequivocal, but unprepared

She left others, me her daughter, the assayers
of personal worth, to stick the pieces
together and recreate her final version,
a faithful reconstruction of what she'd been doing
all her life, the whole picture waiting
for a well-crafted, permanent frame, glass covered

HER SPIRIT AMONG THE COWS (2004)

Last night you furrowed my dreams.
It rained. Cows bellowed even at 3am
calling for their children
crying for grass
moaning about the wetness
the dark, cow solitude, the death of bovines

Cows calling to my mother
reaching out to her through their thick tongues
their plump udders
their grassy bigness
Cows blurting out something elemental
and poignant hour after mournful hour

It was generational, inter-species mayhem banging
on my head, squeezing my heart
sitting on me, crushing both me and my mother at 3am

As though a mountain had toppled
a blur had occurred in the fine tuning
a rainbow had fractured, the spent colours
staining the field, steaming in the crematorium

I tossed and silently groaned
like a clam plucked out of water and thrown
on to dry land. I spent the night
in the vast graveyard where mothers wind up
when their veins collapse

Revisited my mother's house with the doors
both open and locked
her discipline turning into sanctity
the principles and determination like fertilizer
among the clematis and corn stalks

The way you love someone for what they're trying to do
and hate how they go about it
the saint with the cloven hoof and electric eyes

Her last chance came in June to do what she had to
before the earth spilled in her brain
and robins disappeared from her small lonely garden

(written during a low ebb, a drooping flutter of loneliness; at that moment, it felt like all I had in the world was Jenkins, my dog)

TRUE PARTNERSHIP (2004)

One night when the dark had come too early
and nobody called and audible comfort went off the air,
I curled up on the floor with my dog, who was lying there
needy, so needy, I lay down too
on the woolly rug and cupped around him
as though he were the rag doll of my childhood

I heard the poor old woman next door prattle through the wall.
I'm sure televisions and radios everywhere prattled on
while the world lurched about, foundered, recovered, died.

But I ignored all that in the cramped airless space
of my bedroom and drifted off next to the obliging presence
of warm fur, the sweet way he met
my strange interpretation
of loneliness with unresisting collaboration.

Those minutes, that half hour or so of drifting,
the way he slumbered, accepting
my intrusion into his way of being, taking on the template
of combined spirits, as though some innate
instinct arises to say that we're no different when a whimper
calls for a bonding touch.

Some incomprehensible place we flow toward
where it happens, that blurring between dear dog and me:
as though from the first breath,
we're of a oneness –
like radiant stars bound into constellations.

TO MY FATHER ON HIS NINETY FIRST (2005)

I found a card showing a boy and his dogs,
the way they forget time on a sand dune
or a wood or field and lie sleeping
as one fur, one heap of warmth becalmed by sun

And I tried to picture you as that boy
courting the wildflowers in Wisconsin,
down by the river with toads
and the pump by the house and quiet roads
and storms bringing in the green-black sky

I imagine you small with dark curls
around your ears and skinny knees learning
to evolve into athlete's bones,
I wonder how you felt when you came home
to apfel strudel and Germanic do's and don'ts

Alone in the room with the ticking clock
and jars of pickles on the cellar shelf
and Hauser picnics with relatives carved in wood
and farmers bringing in flowers and hay
with old Uncle Albert wobbling on to 105

Where did you find your place in this? Your boy
who followed his pre-recorded singular way
then rebelled for a better life in other states
of being, including Alaska and Connecticut
and those places where 3 children were lain inside
their mother's womb; his wife

And now, the eldest one comes round
to wish her father love and memories that chime
when his 91st year of being invites the sum of us
to gather at the mountain of his life

A PLEA TO MY BROTHER TO BE OBJECTIVE (2006)

You have your reasons, but do you know where they came from?
If you are being honest, how did you assemble the facts?
When did you last feel right about something and happy to hum?
We haven't talked together for years, so why do you give me the axe?

You know so little about me; you've been too distant to bother.
You've pieced together hard-nosed ideas based on conjecture,
then mow me down without kindness in the style of the man I call father.
You assume dominion over all that was mine and drill me with lecture.

I shared space and ideals with our mother for sixteen long years,
did what I could to safeguard our mutual cares and concerns.
Now it's all yours and you make a huge mockery out of my fears;
as though you are right and I am wrong and never a salve for my burns.

We grew up in the care of our mother – -we were sisters and brother.
In time we diverged and went separate ways on treks of our own.
But we still had a share in family lore and kindred memories of each other
So now, why do you reject me and bar the door on the 'family' home?

I WORE NEW KNICKERS ON NEW YEAR'S DAY (2006)

My mother gave me knickers for Christmas.
Not every year, but she kept my bottom covered.
I wore them through egg laying
and the birth of sheep, through earthquakes and tsunamis
divorce, gardening, jogging

I wore them when I moved to England
and carried on between castles and ordinary men.
When my daughter left school
those knickers stayed on me
like an inheritance
or a family heirloom

But now, with my mother gone
and no more new ones coming along
I've had to reassess my role in relation to knickerdom;
the size of my waist
what type of elastic
cotton or nylon
daisies on a white background
or solid red and black. It's up to me now.

I sidle into BHS. Whatever they have,
I'll buy it; none of this fatuous shopping around.
Six pairs of knickers each reduced to £2.
The elastic seems good, the colour's static.
I bring them home and reflect;
it's New Year's Day and new knickers
will always make me think of my mother.

(Voltaire the cat is on his last legs and it breaks my heart to watch him inch slowly downward.)

ON THE WAY OUT (2006)

You wouldn't think one cat would figure in the scheme
of things: bills to pay, war, postal strike, smog in LA,
but when it's yours and you watch him hobble
on his last legs and note the way he sleeps
all day and bumps into things
and eats only a thimble full of meat
and how tiny his turds
the way his constant miaow is now
only a muffled puff of breath

Well, you slow down. You grieve and reflect
on the meaning of life and death,
the purpose of consciousness.

He purrs as he half-attempts to eat
and when I gently fondle the fur holding in his bones,
as though this slow slide toward the one-way door
was merely an ordinary episode
in the provenance of any cat

But why should it be so hard and lagging
and smelly to slide through that primal opening
one last time; what keeps his heart and lungs ticking?
Could it be moonlight or sunlight or rain,
the flutter of the Rayburn in the kitchen?
The security of the little round bed
where he lies moving closer to the edge of the map?

Each morning I dread seeing the further crumblings,
like when his legs folded and he walked on his knees
toward the litter tray and I found him
lying cold and unmoving in his final pee.

I took him covered in a basket to the vet
for a prick in his vein and no memory of the final breath.
His previous small drowsing nearly inseparable from death;
his appearance in death no different from his living one.

(Probably the end of my scanty relationship with my son Michael Henry. We've pulled off the gloves. For whatever reason, all my American family relationships have dissolved into non-communication, indifference, lack of warmth and support, as though every American is an island and must sink or swim on its own—no kindly familiarity allowed)

AMERICAN VISION (2006)

Oh boy of mine
sleep-walking in the dreamland of America.

Buying in and walking out
living the half truths of a whole society

An implanted rib in the cloned body
of a power gone dysfunctional.

Oh American, assuming mastery over the prairies
and common ground of invisible footprints, and still

not perceiving the vast shadow
deflowering elemental reason on the horizon of greed,
not resisting the bloated and self-indulgent;

ignoring your grandmother's accomplishments, Gandhi.
Deaf to the rumblings of whales and the Palestinians.
Asking what sterling is. A castle maybe?

Who would introduce you to Bertrand Russell, Gibran,
Noam Chomsky, Lovelock, St. Exupery?

Do you water your lawn in a drought?
Lock up the safe at night, reject curbs on your liberties?
Oh Sudan, Sahel, smite him who doesn't see!

Slippery fish drowning in a stream of foreign eels,
beating your scales in elation as though you had conquered
currents, but could not swim in the flow of reality

ROWS & ROSE (2007 – for my sister's daughter, Sharon Rose)

Slightly nervous trees line roads that lead toward home,
and that perfect flower of a girl still blooming
tries not to taint her years with modern chrome
and instead confronts the global warming looming

I want them both; the hedgerows and my Rose,
the girl my sister left to search out her way alone.
The lanes and mossy walls, a stream that flows
its path to sea and all that's needed is already known.

Maybe everyone should stand in rows that add
their names to lists; those who don't just eat and sleep
and will carefully fight to save the Rose that's had
her fill of those who merely live like placid sheep

IN MAY HE HAS HIS DAY (2008)

Dear Hans, good man of the day;
all that you say and the way you say it
leads the way to an open door.
That door you have walked through
on one real leg (it's your mind we want more of)
to light, and varied inspirations.
Your mind, a garden of flowering nations
wearing lavender and blue,
a place of wings and chirps and cups
where bees buzz in to sup with you.

So blow those candles out;
be proud of who you are, oh earthly star.
It's not about the number of your limbs
or size of shoe;
it's what you give to all of us
relative to who you are.
And so you fly above the rest
because Earth knows you are a star.

MY FATHER'S 94th (2008)

You've reached Kangchenjunga,
world's 3rd highest peak (Everest is to the left)
and are still upwardly bound.
Oh, the crevasses you've skirted.
Falling boulders, ice sheets, those howling winds
all subverted.
You've talked to the void, the chasm,
the blank wall, the altitude
and there you still are,
climbing in a wheelchair,
ascending through the arts,
the Unitarian church,
the love of a faithful wife.

So on your day in April
when the buds are out
and cake is baking in the oven
and the grandchildren come to test
the steadiness of your knees,
may you feel pleased with yourself
and the varied path you have travelled
in this world, the way you founded
a home for yourself in a hive of faithful bees.

NO SUBSTITUTE (2009)

I forgot one day they would both disappear –
they would leave without saying the password;
This mother and father each in their unique
manner vexing me to walk away, to move my whole
life, including an exemplary dog and borrowed
daughter to my own distant English planet.
Only once when she came to Porlock at Christmas
did the old unfinished diaries wake up
and boil again, spines cracking in the heat.
She went home and threw down her hammer.
He too went underground only recently
like a groundhog allergic to light.
We will never tally each other's tokens again;
the unanswered puzzles will stay hidden
like undug potatoes, like books
buried in trunks in dark, spider-laced attics

SHARON OLDS AND HER MOTHER, ME AND MINE (2009)

My mother on the phone was like a broken
continent wandering from place to place,
not knowing if her voice and body
were in the same zone.
Sharon Old's mother dropped
screaming suddenly in her bedroom;
mine contorted in soon-to-be homeless
blood and faeces in the cold clasp
of her bathtub,
never again to converse
with her cabbages and dwarf corn stalks.
Did she see it coming, this locomotive
of death rounding its last curve?
Maybe she perched in the branches
of the tall eucalyptus and waved
to the sheep below
and feeling closer to God, let go.
She would never have screamed
or even raised her voice;
her migration to Beyond managed
in Quaker fashion – heartbeat silent
in keeping with mute Attenders in her mind.

(Reminiscence about a trip we made to Ireland in 1959 or 1960 while living in Manchester during my mother's exchange teacher interlude.)

MOLES IN WIND (2009)

My mother is up early,
aproned, ladle in hand, her usual
clothes (never sweatshirt or jeans) in the cottage
in Donaghadee; chin out to the wind,
applesauce bubbling on the stove.
We three partial replicas sitting
with our spoons, staring
at boiled eggs, each eggcup a small temple,
the fruit smell wandering
into other rooms.
The coal fire's glowing body waiting
for our attention and words or books.
This is a mother's love song
to our small harmonies nourishing
who she is and how she does it with us
cosy in an Irish friend's house, which I wouldn't
remember so deeply if this arbiter
of coal fires and applesauce and wind
under a slate roof hadn't soothed
me into this unforgettable savoury contentment.

ABERRANT GENES (2009)

He who was once my little brother has stolen my mother
He handled her life to the end and made sure
her addled brain endowed everything she was to him.
Even her most cherished dream fell into ruin
and left him lumbered with foundations and walls
and no sign of the future once built into her plans.
He has robbed me too, a deceit rising in his genes
that moves him to withhold her memories and sighs,
and lock them like ghosts inside the refuge of her walls.
Like a tyrant he has stolen the inner world of her mind,
the secret, unspoken heart copied into diaries
spanning creative years and the continents she travelled;
he has stolen the paper, the ink, stacked her in a cupboard
where her deepest thoughts are denied eyes and light.

That little boy wearing overalls in the photo with Laddie the dog,
the three year old playing in dirt under the arbour
in Santa Cruz, at 11 he wouldn't bare his arms to Italian sun;
who was he really? Did our father's absence
dim a switch that would enable him to tap the truth?

Some undeciphered lack led him to play with the world
for money, as though missing links could be filled in
by Jaguars and land and a wealth of betterments.

But now they're gone, parents and the other sister;
he has only me and property that will stay behind
when his own departure time arrives.
You'd think he'd value our familial connections
even though they can't be banked.

Think of me, send those diaries is all I really ask.
Her release lies in the confused rubble of his mind,
his in growing kinder, mine in being reunited with the past

(To my daughter on her 27th birthday)

HER TWENTY-SEVEN COMPARTMENTS (2009)

First she was one, the tiniest bun.
Then she was two and barely knew
her new mum and dad.
By 3, 4 and 5 I was glad she could speak.
She could run and tweak my alarm.
By 6 what a mix of concerns.
But by 7, 8 and 9 she learns a few rules,
can use a few tools and around 10 she's become a small hen.
Around 12, 13, 14 she's a small snorty fiend
talking back, dribbling the ball
or up in her loft, nose to the wall hiding her food
from the rest of the brood.
From 15 for awhile she loses her style,
goes on the loose like a wild little goose.
So to England we go where at 16 she'll know
there are more lakes to row, so be calm, take it slow.
During 17 she's demure but not always sure which land is best.
So at 18 she heads west back to her nest
leaving her mum lonely and vexed.
At 19 and 20 it's back into school; why? Oh, college is cool!
At 21 she can drink and decide what to think
and act like nobody's fool.
At 22 with Grandma in tow she's back for hello
where Mum lives in Porlock.
But the USA clock calls her back to her job
lest someone should rob what she feels is her space.
During 23 and 24 it's back in for more
and her place in the big money race.
At 25 she's alive, has her own car to drive
and for all of 26 she's a blend and a mix
of college and work, meets the occasional jerk

and studies philosophy. Or is it plutocracy?
27 is now calling; what load is she hauling?
Is she primed for a time when it'll pay to be green
and maybe she'll wean herself off the magical bean
of thinking money's sublime?
Happy birthday to you who I knew as my little girl
but is now a well-spoken pearl who can cook and converse
and generally avoid being daft and adverse.
Bless you, oh daughter of mine.

(On 20 March, at 8:20 am my time, the seldom-heard voice of my brother Jerome called from Staten Island to tell me Pa had passed on. While I sat on my bed weeping, the men's choir of King's College, Cambridge sang a beautifully sad and sombre rendition of a piece by Faure, like a moment of tribute to the ending of my father's life.)

NOW I AM AN ORPHAN (2009)

My father has died and I feel so alone.
A part of my history took its last breath
and has been claimed by the lost past;
my youth, each memory of family,
the family vine pulled down into the dark
permanence of oblivion.

A male choir renders grave choral music by Faure
on the radio and my tears flow like rain.
There is a new hole in the universe.

The sky is grey – its vast blanket
mourning his vanished consciousness.
I wonder how it was for him
as he slid through the final beat of his heart,
the shrinking of all light in his mind . . .
the breath on his lips cooling
into nothingness.

Mary his wife holding a hand
that could no longer respond.;
all his past journeys into spirit and mind,
the flowers and travails of foreign lands
his Alaskan dog, a boat, Mt. McKinley at his back;
laid to rest in the ultimate forgetfulness.

My father has died
and though he has been remote
from me for a long time,
he is now silent and truly gone;
I mourn. inconsolably alone, and grope
for one last squeeze of his arm

SO MUCH FOR THE PASSING (2009)

I cried for a day, then wiped my nose,
stood back and listened. My heart had almost nothing to say.
Old nearly-95 father stopped breathing and I thought well,
why all the fuss when his spent wreck bites the dust;
he never pulled out the plug of his longings or made the pink
camellias of my mind stir with daughterly sentiment.
Cry maybe for scarred babies who never pet a camel
or smell lavender, but this lump of twisted bone
throwing himself out of his bed
and attacking nurses in hospital and at home – -
time for him to head off into the white snow of oblivion.

Funny, I can't remember his laughter
or whether he ever slipped in a joke
or words of comfort and silvers of advice or runes
of beauty about what he believed in
or yearned to know more about or test for its truth.
Whatever he discovered or uncovered, was rarely applied to me.

But his knees grated like mine do now;
above his dark thinning hair, sun-blotched skin, a German tongue.
He had a sweetheart named Grace who died
of ovarian cancer; a strange connection with his own
girls who staved off their ovaries
and gave birth to only one babe each, and offered them to others.

May he leave for me in death what he never gave
while he had breath. Earn it, always came out
of his Calvinist mouth. Only during my marriage
did he treat me (or was it my spouse?) as an equal mind.

No, he dropped my young hand;
took my puppy on a long hike and came back without it,
berated me for wearing sexy clothes when he came to visit;
we never amiably conversed, he never listened.

You poor damned man, searching for the scent of your being
while closing doors on things you fear or dread;
you managed by punching the keys of acceptability.
From the gulf between us, I never glimpsed
you at anchor in a single haven of warmth other than your wife.
Now rest in peace, you lonely set of bones.

BE MORE UTILITARIAN (2009)

My dead father's wife sounds like somebody
on a throne bossing the serfs;
anything that might dent her kingdom she spurns
me with; I'm a persistent flea in her dog's ear.

I've reached a strange point about what it all adds up to
so far; this great aloneness in the world.
One by one the loss of family, like rabbits picked
off by wolves; one adopted little rose bush who's really not
mine. So where am I?
Me and the earth, the earth saying
strip away the unwanted, the unnecessary, unused; obey
only the deep-down final voice, the last
calling, follow your essential track, the line of reasoning
you can't ignore. Peel down
the desultory layers right to your pith,
that undeniable essential core.
In all the swirling flotsam, find the hard
rock of the steady who-you-are. . .and be faithful.

But the thought of infinity, silence, cold space, the end
quells me. Then I have a mug of tea
and come back thinking: do what you can, let the rest happen,
be true to your spirit, mist, barnacles, heaven. . .
I will weave together the missing figures in my tableau:
family, money, a house, help, massage, jokes, a publisher, an old
confidante
as though they were nervous monkeys to figure out and befriend.

So, I hear whispered, grow a little tomato plant.
Buy my good dog a bone.
See the mist as a thin dress safeguarding sanctity

(I'm going through a very strange personal set of rooms; as though I don't even know what house I'm in or what I'm made of or where I'm going. It's all stiff neck, dark thoughts floating out of my head, a sense of being led by something unfathomable and unfamiliar. I decide to put away the wine.)

COMING TO FRUITION (2009)

The stems springing out of her will be
watered and gathered
by those who tend the world
of poetry. An unknown hand lifts
the watering can.
Plants without names sprout unexpected leaves
and flowers evolve into food with no name –
a strange garden in Devon's red earth
where before a decipherable patch grew
but sat unpicked by any wise gardener.
She's poised between serviceable
weed and precious blooms still laced
with shade, but waiting,
always waiting to be gathered.
Something new planted in her from the outside
shows petals of good timing
and stems that won't break in the wind.
Her fruit will finally be recognized
for its depth of flavour on the tongue.

REKNITTING (2009)

Whatever decides, the Great Programme, spiritual license,
reverberating motes – I need another lifetime to carry me
down through the lace of fields and slant of hills,
the finding of my gull self flying partially horizontal
above the coast path and the animal-excluding golf courses,
through the silver of silence when the moon is full.
I need to understand a bear, a wolf, a rook,
a rabbit watching seasons through stems and roots.
I need the embrace of proud summits
in Snowdonia and like Stanley, find Livingstone
at the top of a river without a name.
At night I gaze into the simmering heart of a coal fire
while my feet dream of pressing all over the outer Hebrides.
Talk to trees. Learn sea. These things take years.
To see beyond the mountain is a rare art.
Knit, knit. Undo the weak stitches, the snarled path,
reknit my relationship with the vacuum cleaner, ask
whether there's a necessity for wine. Change from synthetic
to wool. Write a book that carries me into a world
where I can then reappear in the turning of pages.
Learn resilience; the bouncing back of a drained heart,
the mind stopping to rest in the clasp of doing nothing.
I will circle the earth 100 years from now, float through time
watching progress; do the lily and dormouse still exist,
do humans gaze at stars? What can I bring with me
in a journey through the universe, telling stories as I go,
gathering connections, rounding up the lost and torn?
Who out there dwells on such things, or am I alone?